ROCCO'S CLAMS
A FINANCIAL FABLE

— Walter John Erb III —

Drawings by Jack Wiens

ISBN: 1481183389
ISBN 13: 9781481183383

In a very special place filled with make believe and truth lives a young horse named Rocco. Rocco spends most of his days working on the farm with his father, mother, and sister. In return, they are provided plenty of grass and grain to eat, water to drink, and a place to live. After his work is completed each day, Rocco plays in the fields with his friends.

Rocco knows what is required of him, but it is hard work, and the sun is hot in the summer, and in the winter the air is cold.

"I wish I didn't have to spend all this time working here on the farm." Rocco would consider this each day as he completed his chores. He dreamed of a life where the grass and grain tasted better, the water was colder, and there were no chores that were required of him.

One evening after a hard day's work, while playing in the fields outside of the farm, Rocco and his friend Charlie decided to go for a long walk in search of adventure. They headed farther down the path toward the mountains than they had ever gone before. After a long gallop, they came to the base of the mountains.

"Should we climb the mountain?" Charlie asked.

"Certainly, it will be fun," Rocco responded, as he was always looking for challenges and something new.

After a long climb, they reached the top and found the mountain was flat, with lots of trees, grass, apple orchards, piles of grain, and small lakes of sparkling blue. As they gazed on this newfound place, two other young horses came trotting toward them.

"This is the greatest place in the world!" one of the horses exclaimed.

"What is this place?" Rocco asked.

"This is the Hill of the Clams where you can have whatever you want and all your dreams come true!" proclaimed the first horse quite proudly.

"She's right! Just ask the clams," the second horse announced as they trotted past them and back down the side of the mountain.

Rocco and Charlie wondered what that meant, but realized their time playing in the fields and the journey to this location had taken the whole afternoon. "Let's come back tomorrow," Rocco said to Charlie. They turned and headed home with a new excitement for what they would discover the next day.

Rocco ran home and could not wait to tell his sister. When he entered the stables, he began to tell her about the wonderful place he and Charlie had just found. Rocco's sister stood in her stable munching on a pile of hay that was placed in the corner. Rocco could tell she did not appreciate the interruption as she did not bother to stop eating and responded with muffled words. "What place?" she replied.

Rocco continued to explain. "We found a mountaintop with blue lakes, piles of grain, and the greenest grass we have ever seen."

"What more could a horse wish for that you do not already have?" his sister asked in a sarcastic tone. He could sense that she was mocking him, and knew he needed to prove it to her. He left his sister to finish her meal and headed to his stall for the evening.

The next day Rocco woke up early with the thought of the hilltop on his mind. He ran out of the stables, down the path, and away toward the hills, neglecting his daily chores. The mountains provided an amazing view in the early morning sunlight, but all Rocco could think about was the adventures that he would find that day.

He came to the base of the mountain and searched for the same path they had taken the evening before. He knew he should have waited for Charlie, but he wanted to return as soon as possible and was too impatient to wait for him. Once he found the path, he started his trip up the mountain.

As he walked, he noticed pictures on signposts that he and Charlie had not seen the evening before as it was late and the light was low in the path beneath the trees. The pictures displayed well-dressed horses, beautiful lakes and waterfalls, fancy carriages pulled by elegant stallions, and gorgeous mares with beads strung through their manes.

Rocco began trotting faster and faster until he reached the final sign at the top of the hill that read, "*Welcome To Our Hill.*" He trotted along the path lined with tall evergreen trees. *Wow!* he thought to himself, *This must be heaven.* He was mesmerized by the amazing sights, sounds, and smells. "What an incredible place I have found!" he blurted out loud as he stopped for a short while to look around. Way off in the distance he could see the ocean, and in the other direction he thought he could see his own farm. Rocco felt as if he was on top of the world.

Rocco strolled across one of the green meadows until he came to a large lake. He was thirsty, so he stopped to take a drink. As he leaned down, he heard a voice from under the water say, "If you drink this water, payment will be required."

Rocco stepped back, wondering where the voice had come from. He peered down into the water and saw a small clam slowly moving toward the surface. When the clam emerged his voice became clear and understandable. "Mr. Horse," the clam began. "If you want to drink this water—and believe me, it is the best water you will ever taste—you will need to do one simple thing." Rocco nodded in agreement as he was very thirsty and now wanted to have a drink of this water, especially if it was the best water he would taste. "What do I need to do?" he asked. The clam responded, "You must carry me on your back to the ocean and set me free at the water's edge."

Rocco looked up to see the ocean way off in the distance. He thought for a few seconds and then agreed. Rocco knelt down beside the water's edge and allowed the clam to climb on top of his back. The clam jumped out of the water, opened his mouth and clamped down on Rocco's long, dark brown mane on the back of his neck.

This did not seem to be too difficult a task, Rocco thought. He took a long drink from the clear lake filled with cold water. "That clam was right!" he muttered out loud as water spilled out the sides of his mouth, "This is the best water I have ever tasted." He believed that this drink of water was worth a trip to the beach to release the clam, so away he went down the other side of the mountain. As he galloped along, he could barely feel the little clam bouncing up and down on the back of his neck. He knew the clam had a tight hold of his mane, but he did not realize how tight it was until he reached the ocean.

"We are here, Mr. Clam," Rocco announced. He turned back to see the clam still holding tightly to the long strands of hair.

The clam muttered something and Rocco listened intently to understand what he was saying. "You have to pull me off and throw me in the water!" the clam declared as best he could with his mouth closed tight.

Rocco had a difficult time understanding and asked the clam to repeat it. By the third attempt, he finally understood and reached back to free the clam from his mane. Rocco carefully placed the little clam between his teeth and began to pull, but the little creature had a powerful grip. Finally, after several more attempts he was able to pull the clam free. He swung his head to the side and tossed the little clam into the ocean. Rocco never heard another word from the clam as it slipped below the water's surface.

Rocco had traveled quite a distance to the beach and used a lot of effort to release the clam. He wondered if the long journey was worth the drink of water. During his long walk back he began to think about the delicious water. The thought of it began to make him thirsty again, and by the time he had reached the top of the mountain he was ready for another drink.

Rocco approached the edge of the lake and looked deep into the water to see if more clams were waiting. Rocco did not see anything so he stretched his neck, took a few sips, and then stopped to look around. He did not see anything and believed he was able to finish his drink undetected. He leaned toward the water and took a long drink. When Rocco finished drinking, he lifted his head and this time, he saw something move on the edge of the lake that startled him.

There on the bank were three clams staring at him. The largest clam spoke. "You know the price for drinking this water, and you took two very *large* drinks." Rocco knew the answer but remained silent while the large clam continued. "You need to carry all three of us down to the ocean and release us."

Rocco stared at them for a few seconds with the taste of the cold, wonderful water still in his mouth. Before they could jump onto his back, Rocco said, "I need to know how long I can keep you on my back before I let you go."

The largest clam responded, "You can keep us on your back as long as you want, but I would not recommend it." Before Rocco could ask why, the clams jumped high into the air and grabbed tightly to his mane. He took off for the ocean once again, and as he did, he looked up at the sun and realized it was already noon. He had spent half of his day drinking from the mountain lake and taking four clams for a ride on his back to the ocean.

Rocco reached the beach and jumped into the ocean water hoping the clams would release their hold. *No luck,* he thought while swimming and splashing, thinking the sounds of the ocean water would cause them to let go, but they kept their hold and refused to fall into the ocean.

Rocco repeated the same process as he did with the first clam. Pain surged through his neck as the clams held tight. After tugging and pulling, the clam finally began to release, and after quite a struggle, Rocco had him free. "You are free, Mister Clam," Rocco said, dropping the clam into the water. He watched as the clam pushed himself along and began moving farther away into deeper water. He hoped he would hear the clam thank him for the trip this time, but the clam didn't say a word as it disappeared into the waves.

Rocco worked for another hour on the remaining clams. Once they were released, he turned back and headed toward home. He was tired and frustrated at this point and began to wonder if this new adventure was worth the effort. He trudged along and reached his stable just before the sun was about to set. Within a few minutes he was fast asleep, but he dreamed of the water he had tasted that day. When he awoke the next morning, he was ready to head back to the Hill of the Clams.

Rocco decided to let the clams he gathered stay on his back for the day and then take them to the beach all at once. He trotted over to a field of wonderful smells. Clover and tall grass of the greenest color he had ever seen covered the field. Apple orchards and piles of grain were located at all four corners of the pasture. The sight of this made Rocco hungry, as he had not yet had his breakfast.

He approached the gate to go inside and was met at the entrance by another clam. Rocco stopped and waited for the clam's instructions. "You will need to provide transportation for thirty clams for entering the field."

Rocco's stomach growled as he stared out at the clover, apples, and grain. He agreed to the clam's conditions and entered through the gate.

What a treat he had just discovered! After he filled his belly, he began to run and play in the fields. When he returned to the gate to leave, the clams were waiting for him. Rocco bent down, allowing the clams to jump on his back. He went back to the lake for one more drink of water. When he finished, he decided that he would wait until tomorrow before going back to the beach. He remained on the top of the mountain for the remainder of the day before heading home.

Rocco's mother was waiting for him when he arrived. "Where have you been, Rocco? And what is on your back?" she asked in a scolding voice.

Rocco looked at the ground as he quietly uttered a response. "I was on the mountain beyond the fields where I found these clams," he said as his mother strained to hear his words.

Rocco's mother looked at the clams and then declared, "Rocco, you must stay away from the Hill of the Clams! It is a dangerous place, especially for a young horse like you."

Rocco lifted his head and looked his mother straight in the eye. "I am not a young horse. I know what I'm doing!" he said, a bit upset. His mother shrugged in disappointment and turned, leaving Rocco alone for the night.

Rocco woke up early the next morning, ignored his chores once again, and returned to the hill, where he spent the entire day playing, eating, and drinking from the lake. By the end of the day, he had over two hundred clams piled on his back. The clams filled his mane and clanked together as he walked home that evening. He had no energy left, and the day was too far gone for him to take any of the clams to the ocean. *Besides,* he thought, *what harm could there be in keeping them one more night?*

The next morning, Rocco discovered there were more clams than the day before. Many new clams were holding tight to his mane. Rocco realized that keeping the clams on his back for any length of time would simply mean more clams would be there for him to take to the ocean and it would be more work to free them.

After that, he left each day with good intentions of returning to the ocean, but with each visit to the hill, he would make some excuse as to why he could not go to the beach, and after several weeks the number of clams on his back and tail grew larger until his entire mane and tail were *completely* covered. In all this time he had not seen his friend Charlie and wondered where he had been.

Again Rocco returned home and entered the stable before his mother could see how many clams were attached to him. He slipped by his sister, who was already fast asleep, and as he turned the corner he bumped into his father.

"Where have you been, Rocco?" he asked. Rocco remained quiet, again staring at the floor of the stable, pushing some of the hay around with his hoof. His father continued, "Looks like you didn't listen to your mother's advice and you returned to the Hill of the Clams." Rocco refused to look up and kept his head low. "Well, you and I need to make a trip to a nearby farm. We will be gone for several weeks." Rocco could hear his father's words were firm, so he continued to listen without looking up at his father. "That should keep you away from that place."

His father finished and turned to head back to his stall. As he started to leave, Rocco blurted out, "But Father, I need to return to the ocean before—"

His father interrupted. "Sorry, Rocco, you must go with me. You have ignored your chores long enough. This trip will help you make up for the work you have missed here at home."

Rocco and his father left for their journey the next morning. Rocco's mother and sister watched them leave. The clams on Rocco's back and tail made strange noises as they bumped into each other. He began to worry and knew he needed to return to the ocean to free the many clams before the problem was too big, but he was unable to return until he and his father had completed their task.

Weeks later, when Rocco and his father returned home, his mother and sister were quite surprised to see what had become of Rocco. The clams covered his entire body except for his face. Rocco trailed far behind his father, as he could barely walk. The weight was too much as he slowly and carefully took each step.

His mother ran over to him, "Rocco, where did all these clams come from, and why are there so many?"

Rocco looked at his mother with a sad expression. "I should have listened to your advice, but I kept going back to the hill of clams." He paused as a shudder of pain ran through his back as some of the clams tightened their hold. "Now they have multiplied and covered every part of me."

His mother could tell that Rocco was ashamed, and she was also concerned for Rocco's health.

"Do they hurt?" his sister asked. Rocco nodded and slowly walked past them to his stall. He was extremely tired from the trip and needed to rest.

The next morning, after a restless night and before the sun was above the horizon, without telling anyone where he was going, Rocco headed out of the stable and toward the ocean. His legs shook with pain, and he stumbled and fell on several occasions. He was so focused on each step that he did not hear Charlie walking up behind him.

"Rocco, is that you?" Charlie asked as he came up beside Rocco.

Rocco turned his head in shame. "Don't look at me!" he said, afraid of what his friend would think.

"What happened to you, Rocco, and where did all these clams come from?"

Rocco, still showing his embarrassment, kept his head turned away from Charlie and mumbled his explanation. Charlie did his best to hear what his friend had to say. "They came from the Hill of the Clams. I must return to the ocean at once to get rid of them," Rocco said, knowing he needed to explain the danger to Charlie, although Charlie could easily see the results of spending too much time on the hill.

Charlie responded, "Rocco, when I told my parents about the hill of the clams, they would not let me return with you and kept me busy on the farm for these past several weeks." Charlie looked at his friend with a sad expression. "I see why they didn't let me go with you." Charlie continued to examine all the clams on Rocco's back and let out a sigh of relief, realizing his parents had made the right decision in keeping him away from the hill of clams.

Rocco finally turned to face his friend. "Now I wish I had not gone to that place and had stayed home too."

"Is there anything I can do to help?" Charlie asked.

Rocco just shook his head. "No, I need to fix this," he said, then slowly walked away. Charlie watched as Rocco trudged toward the mountains.

Rocco was humiliated and sad that his friend had seen him in this condition. *What did I get myself into?* he thought as he continued along the path, trying not to think about the pain that grew worse with every step.

It was not until midday, when the sun was high, that Rocco arrived on the sandy beach of the ocean. He struggled to keep his balance as he stepped into the soft sand and tried to keep from falling with each step toward the water's edge. "This will be the hard part," he said aloud as he turned his head and grabbed the first clam from his back and began to pull. He knew this was going to be the toughest challenge he would ever face.

By the time the sun was about to set, Rocco had pulled only thirty clams from the hundreds waiting for their freedom. The clams had been holding on so tightly that some pulled out his hair, revealing his skin when he removed them. He bled a little from some of the places they had once been. He tried hard to fight back tears, but it was no use. He began to cry as he stood there in the fading sunlight. He was tired and hungry and just wanted to be normal again, but knew he must go on or the clams would multiply again and his day's work would be lost.

Rocco stayed on the beach late into the night, struggling to pull off as many clams as he could, until exhaustion overtook him and he collapsed. Early in the morning, Rocco felt a gentle nudge and thought he was dreaming, but opened his eyes to see an old grey horse standing above him. Startled, Rocco pulled himself up and tried to focus on the stranger. "Who are you?" Rocco asked.

The old horse simply looked him over, shook his head, and said, "I see you've spent too much time on the hill of the clams." The stranger circled Rocco, staring at all the clams that covered his body.

"You know about the Hill of the Clams?" Rocco asked.

"Of course I do," the stranger responded. "I was once in the same situation as you."

Rocco's face lit up. "You were? How did you free yourself of all the clams?" He anxiously waited for the answer, as hundreds of clams still clung tightly to him.

"Two weeks!" was all the old horse said as he continued to look at all of the clams. "It took me two weeks of hard work to remove them."

The old horse let out a short laugh, then gave Rocco even more bad news. "Of course, I did not have as many clams on my body as you."

"Two weeks?" Rocco asked in a voice of complete disappointment. "Don't you have any good suggestions for me or any way you can help me get rid of these clams faster?" Rocco was desperate at this point and was hoping the stranger had a quick and fast way to help him.

"Sorry, boy," the old horse answered. "My recommendation is that you take your time, don't get frustrated, and once you remove the clams, remember the amount of work required to handle each clam, and be more careful in the future."

Rocco huffed and shrugged, knowing he was in for a long and painful ordeal.

The old horse turned to leave, but then stopped and turned his head with one final piece of advice. "Try getting rid of the large clams first, as they will be the first to multiply." He looked Rocco over one more time to see where the large clams were on Rocco's body. "Also, pull hard, but slow, and you will keep from hurting yourself as much as you are now."

Rocco nodded in agreement. He searched out the largest clam he could find and began pulling.

Day turned to night and then night to day, and Rocco continued working on the clams. He would only rest for small periods of time, and after a week of remaining on the beach; he had removed only a small section of the clams from his mane. He realized he would be here much longer than two weeks.

His stomach was rumbling and he needed to eat. He decided to go home for a short time, let his family know where he was, and then return until the task was complete. As he made his way home, he again passed over the hill of clams and stopped to admire the crystal clear lake and beautiful green pasture, but even with the pain of hunger in his stomach he turned away and continued his journey toward home.

When Rocco arrived, his family greeted him at the gate. Rocco's father was the first to speak. "Rocco, you should have at least let us know where you were for so long."

Rocco kept his courage and looked his dad in the eye. "I know, Dad," he responded. "I was in a hurry to get back to the beach to get rid of these clams."

His mother came close to Rocco and looked at the areas where he had removed the clams. "Rocco, you're hurt," she said as she turned Rocco into the light to see where he had pulled the hair from his body. While his mother examined Rocco, Rocco's father asked him a question. "Are you going back, son?"

Rocco was quick to answer. "Yes. I need to continue before they multiply."

His father agreed and realized that his son had learned a valuable lesson. He gave Rocco some encouragement and then let him know that he and his mother would visit every other day and would bring him food and water. Rocco gave a small smile and turned back toward the stables, went inside, had a small meal, and fell asleep.

Rocco woke up late the next morning and felt the pain of the remaining clams. He looked across his back, belly, and legs to discover several new clams. He sighed and headed out toward the ocean with determination to get rid of them once and for all. Rocco reached the ocean's edge and immediately went back to work, paying close attention to remove the largest clams first.

Two more weeks went by, and he could see he was making good progress but still had quite a bit of work to do. His parents kept their promise, and every two days they pulled a small cart of hay, grain, and fresh water to the beach.

His back and belly were hurting, but the weight of the clams had been greatly diminished. He continued pulling and tugging and releasing the clams. As he worked, he realized this work was much greater than anything he had ever had to do on the farm.

After spending a total of five weeks on the beach, he reached the end of his task and pulled the remaining clams from his front leg. With a final toss, he heard the last clam splash into the ocean. Of all of the hundreds of clams he released, not one of them had thanked him for what he had done. He was bleeding and had lost a good portion of his mane and tail. He was exhausted.

As he turned away from the water's edge, he was greeted by the old horse. "I hope you learned your lesson, boy."

Rocco nodded. "Yes, sir, I did! I will *never* again return to the hill of clams."

The old horse smiled. "There is nothing wrong with giving a clam or two a ride to the ocean every now and then, but I've seen many horses end up like you....Including me. It is not the clams that present the problem, but those who cannot control their desire for what the clams offer." The old horse continued, "Just remember this day, and understand that the water and grass taste the same in your meadow as they do on the hill of clams."

Rocco thought for a moment and realized the old horse was right. Still, he did not need the clams any longer and promised himself to stay *far away* from that hill.

The old horse was glad to see Rocco was in much better shape than when he had seen him weeks before. They said goodbye and Rocco began heading home. This time, he carried no clams, and he was much wiser.

As the next few weeks passed, the hair on Rocco's tail and mane grew back, and eventually Rocco returned to the playful horse he once was. He had learned a valuable lesson, and every evening as he and Charlie played in the fields he would look out in the distance at the mountains and remember the burden he had once carried. Rocco never again returned to the mountain, and instead worked for the things he wanted and needed without the help of a single clam.

Several principles have been presented in this story. The clams represent *debt*, which is easy to acquire but can be quite difficult to remove. Rocco's ability to work on the farm and receive the same benefits he received on the hill of clams demonstrates ***immediate payment for goods or services***. ***Interest from debt***, the last principle revealed in the story, is demonstrated through the multiplication of the clams on Rocco's body.

Debt, a growing concern for individuals, families, cities, states, our federal government, and countries around the world, reveals a lack of spending control—as was the case for Rocco. It is all too obvious that we are a society who would rather have now and pay tomorrow, than work and save now for the special things we would like to have tomorrow.

Consider the modern family—in most cases, the amount of income is revealed by the amount of debt the family holds. As income increases, so does the amount of clams that are piled onto the family's back. A larger house, better car, and nicer things, most of which are paid for with a larger mortgage, loans, or credit card debt, are all based on what can be paid month to month as the debt reflects the income. Certain limits of debt are beneficial and sometimes necessary, but so many find themselves going well beyond these limits.

The reality in this story was that Rocco was much better off working and immediately paying for the things he needed and wanted on the farm. Rocco had discovered this debt provided immediate satisfaction, but caused him a significant amount of added labor and stress in the long run. As interest accrues on our debt, there is an increased amount of work involved and an extended payback of that debt. The sooner young people realize this, the better off they will be, as they will be equipped to deal with the bombardment of offers, allowing them to receive immediate satisfaction with a delayed payback of the debt, with interest.

The principle of **immediate payment for goods and services** is difficult for many adults to adhere to, and the trend is passed along to their children. Demonstrating this concept in our lives will help establish wise habits in the lives of our children. Having and using the various credit cards in our possession causes us to feel like our income is higher than we actually receive. If we make fifty thousand dollars a year and place ten thousand on our credit cards in that same year without removing it immediately, we are living as if we have made sixty thousand dollars. This increases the standard of living in the short term, but eventually reduces the standard of living in the long run. This pattern becomes dangerous, as Rocco discovered.

Provide the tools necessary for young people to learn and practice these habits. You could begin with a set of chores for which your children are paid every week or give them a weekly allowance. We decided to help our children through practice and established a system in which they were provided three envelopes, the first was labeled "giving" and was for them to give a set amount of their earnings to our church or a charity of their choice. The second was labeled "savings," and the last envelope was labeled "spend." With each payday, they would place their money into the various envelopes, and they began to properly allocate their earnings and save for the things they wanted. We hope this practice remains with them long into the future.

The final principle is *interest from debt*. Rocco learned the hard way that the clams on his body would multiply and continue to become a larger burden. If he removed the clams immediately, the problem was resolved, but if he left them on his back for any length of time, they would begin growing and would eventually increase in number.

The old horse told Rocco that giving a clam or two a ride to the ocean was OK, and the same holds true for us. Having a credit card is not a bad thing, and hopefully, if we use them, we can learn to pay them off right away. If we allow the debt to remain on the credit cards, we subject ourselves to the interest that will be added to the amount we owe. Just as Rocco allowed too many clams on his back and then took too long to remove them, we will encounter the same experience as the debt will grow and multiply (***interest from debt***). The best way to avoid this interest is to avoid the debt altogether.

Let's help our children learn the benefits of avoiding debt early in life and keep them from learning through trial and error. Let them know that certain debt is beneficial and may be necessary—such as a mortgage, student loans, and reasonably borrowing to own a vehicle—and what debt should be avoided.

Sadly enough, in today's American society, many families hold too much debt, mainly credit card debt, which averages between six thousand and fifteen thousand dollars per family. This debt continues to weigh down folks and has slowed their pace, or is keeping them from making any personal economic advancement.

At first Rocco did not understand the danger to which he had exposed himself. He was able to release the few clams right away, and no harm had occurred. As time progressed, he became caught in the snare of spending, debt, and interest, causing him to become overburdened.

Helping your children develop proper spending habits and a strong awareness of debt's consequences is the purpose of this book. Perhaps they will always keep this story in their memory and when the desire for that special item arises, which is beyond their spending ability, they will remember Rocco and his clams.

Our two daughters, Jenna and Julia, were introduced to this story at ages eleven and thirteen. The best part of sharing such a story occurs when they understand the concepts and begin applying the meaning to true-life.

Our family currently lives in Dallas, Texas, and occasionally visits the large malls located in this area. During one of the busy holiday seasons, we walked into one of the largest malls in the city of Dallas. My youngest daughter stared wide-eyed at all the festive decorations and myriad of stores surrounding us. She turned to me and, with a serious tone of voice, said, "Dad, *this* is the hill of the clams."

Needless to say, she had applied the story to the situation we were facing. Although there is nothing wrong with visiting and shopping at the mall, she had already realized the danger that was present, and for the rest of our visit both Jenna and Julia made certain that we did not pile an excessive amount of clams onto our backs.

I certainly hope this story has helped provide a clear understanding in an easy manner for your child. This story, the second in the series, plants financial planning seeds for our children, which can grow and be used for the remainder of their lives, and can be passed along to future generations.

If you liked this story, look for the first in this series, titled *Junior's Fishpond*—a fable that will help your child develop an understanding of Retirement Planning. Look for other financial fables to become available in the near future that, in all, will play a part in building pictures within young minds that will help develop proper financial planning habits.

These stories are recommended for children nine years of age and older.

Jack Wiens

Jack has had a love for art since childhood, when he filled tablets with drawings of cowboys, Indians, soldiers, monsters, and cars. His childhood dream was to work for Disney, but for now he is happily illustrating children's books.

He was born in Oregon, grew up in Southern California, and has lived in Missouri, Colorado, and has returned to Oregon where he currently resides. He is a grandpa to three wonderful grandchildren and loves nature, riding his bike, playing tennis, and exploring new places. Besides his work as an artist, Jack works with others to help them develop their creativity, as his additional time is devoted to providing art workshops and classes.